MG 5.6 .5pt.

EDGE
BOOKS™

KILLER JOBS!

HISTORY'S MOST DANGEROUS JOBS

BY SUZANNE GARBE

T 40870

CAPSTONE PRESS
a capstone imprint

Edge Books are published by Capstone Press,
1710 Roe Crest Drive, North Mankato, Minnesota 56003
www.capstonepub.com

Library of Congress Cataloging-in-Publication Data
Garbe, Suzanne.
  Killer jobs!: history's most dangerous jobs / by Suzanne Garbe.
    pages cm. — (Edge books. Dangerous history)
  Includes bibliographical references and index.
  Summary: "Describes in detail several of history's most dangerous
jobs"—Provided by publisher.
Audience: Age 11
Audience: Grade 4 to 6
ISBN 978-1-4765-0127-7 (library binding)
ISBN 978-1-4765-3383-4 (ebook pdf)
1. Hazardous occupations—Juvenile literature. I. Title.
HD7262.G378 2014
331.702—dc23   2013009480

Editorial Credits
Mandy Robbins, editor; Sarah Bennett, designer; Marcie Spence,
media researcher; Jennifer Walker, production specialist

Photo Credits
Bridgeman Art Library: 7, Ken Welsh, 10; Getty Images: Chip Chipman/
Bloomberg, 27, Lewis W. Hine/Buyenlarge, 17, Lewis W. Hine/George Eastman
House, 25, Maxim Marmur/AFP, 21, Popperfoto, 15, 23, Time Life Pictures/
Mansell, 9, 19; Shutterstock: Action Sports Photography, 5, Amgun, design
element, BortN66, cover (top left), Charmaine A Harvey, 13, David Hyde,
cover (bottom left), Evgeniyqw, 1, lolloj, design element, luigi nifosi, cover
(bottom right), Oliver Sved, 28-29, Tyler Olson, cover (top right), Valentin
Agapov, design element

Printed in the United States of America in Stevens Point, Wisconsin.
032013   007227WZF13

TABLE OF CONTENTS

OCCUPATIONAL HAZARDS

Scaling 200-foot (61-meter) cell phone towers. Racing cars at speeds of more than 200 miles (322 kilometers) per hour. Sailing through raging ocean waves in the hunt for fresh fish. It's all in a day's work. Some dangerous jobs have obvious risks. Other deadly jobs may surprise you. You might assume a particular job, such as leading a country, is safe—until you look through the history books.

Many countries keep statistics that show how dangerous different jobs are. Historians have also studied jobs from the past to figure out the risks workers have faced over time. What jobs throughout history have been the most dangerous? You might be surprised.

Race car drivers Brian Scott and Steve Wallace collide during a 2010 NASCAR race.

PYRAMID BUILDER

Huge pyramids have stood in the desert of Egypt for more than 4,000 years. The pyramids were built as **tombs** for Egypt's **pharaohs**. The largest pyramid is as tall as a 48-story building.

The pyramids were huge construction projects. People across Egypt helped build them. Paid workers included craftsmen, villagers, and peasants. Although the workers were treated well, the work was hard on their bodies. Nearby burial sites reveal that workers' bones showed evidence of **arthritis**. Broken skulls, arms, and legs were also common. When the pyramids were built, upper-class Egyptians lived to be 50 or 60 years old. Pyramid workers lived to be only 35 or 40.

FACT

For years, people wondered how the pyramids were built. One of the strangest suggestions was that aliens built them.

tomb—a grave, room, or building that holds a dead body

pharaoh—a king of ancient Egypt

arthritis—a disease that makes people's bone joints swollen and painful

Pyramid builders hauled stone blocks weighing 2.5 to 15 tons (2.3 to 13.6 metric tons) each.

ROMAN PRAEGUSTATORE

Modern media reports don't include many stories of people dying by poison. But history is filled with them, especially in Roman times (753 BC to AD 476). Husbands and wives poisoned each other. Business people poisoned their rivals. Wealthy, powerful Romans were often targeted by their enemies.

Some wealthy Romans protected themselves from poison. From about 330 BC to AD 450, high-class Romans had people test their food for poison. There was only one way to test it back then—by eating it. The food testers, called praegustatores (PRAY-gus-tay-tuhrs), were sometimes paid servants. Other times they were slaves. The praegustatore would take the first bite of every meal. If he or she was okay, the wealthy person knew the food was safe to eat. Eating food may not sound like a tough job, but praegustatores risked their lives at every meal.

FACT

The word *praegustatore* is a combination of two Latin words. *Prae* means "before." The verb *gusto* means "to taste."

8

Wealthy Romans often had bountiful feasts.

EUROPEAN ROYALTY

In 2011 a University of Cambridge history professor in England figured out history's most dangerous job: European king or queen. Between the years 600 and 1800, almost one out of every four European kings and queens died violent deaths. Fifteen percent of them were murdered. That's even higher than the risk faced by soldiers fighting in wars today.

Being leaders in certain countries and time periods was especially dangerous. Between 889 and 1094, 15 out of 17 Scottish kings were killed. Norway had seven kings from 1103 to 1162. All seven were killed. Usually, kings and queens were killed by other people who wanted the throne. Other times they were killed by rival leaders of other countries.

UNITED STATES
PRESIDENTS
IN PERIL

Of the 44 U.S. presidents, four of them have been murdered. This means that about 9 percent of American presidents have been killed. The second deadliest job in the United States is commercial fishing. In 2010 only 0.12% of fishing workers were killed on the job. That makes being the U.S. president more than 75 times more deadly than commercial fishing.

The U.S. presidents who have been murdered are:

Abraham Lincoln in 1865 (16th president)

James Garfield in 1881 (20th president)

William McKinley in 1901 (25th president)

John F. Kennedy in 1963 (35th president)

the murder of King Richard II

WASTE PICKER

For thousands of years, people have dug through trash to reuse and recycle materials. These people are known as waste pickers. Today waste pickers earn money by selling paper, plastic, and metal to recyclers.

Being a waste picker is dangerous to a person's health. In many countries, waste pickers live in or near garbage dumps. These dumps are filled with **toxic** liquids and gases. Waste pickers are more likely to suffer from diseases such as cancer and asthma. Babies born to mothers who are waste pickers are more likely to have health problems too.

"I vomited so much. I got there and I thought 'God, why do I have to do this type of work?' I didn't think I'd ever have to do something like this for a living."

— Durga Mukherjee, a waste picker in New Delhi, India

toxic—poisonous

Waste pickers in South Africa save useful items, such as boards, to sell.

PANAMA CANAL CONSTRUCTION WORKER

Throughout history, people have used ships to transport items around the world. The continents of North and South America posed a challenge before 1914. To ship goods from the Atlantic Ocean to the Pacific Ocean, ships had to sail around South America. This was a long, dangerous, expensive trip.

In 1880 the French government tried to fix the problem. They started building a **canal** through the country of Panama. The canal would cut the trip down by about 8,000 miles (12,875 km). About 20,000 canal workers died from diseases spread by mosquitos, such as malaria and yellow fever. The French gave up in 1889.

In 1904 the U.S. government began building the canal where the French left off. Officials kept working conditions clean and sprayed for mosquitos. Their efforts resulted in 75 percent fewer deaths than the French effort. Still, about 5,600 Americans died building the canal. Another 38,000 workers got sick each year. The medicine to treat malaria made some workers lose their hearing. Between the French and American efforts, more than 25,000 workers died building the Panama Canal.

Workers building the Panama Canal faced hot, wet conditions.

canal—a channel that is dug across land; canals join bodies of water so that ships can travel between them

COAL MINER

Coal has been a major source of power around the world since the late 1700s. It has been used to cook food, power steam engines, and run power plants. But coal mining comes at a cost.

Coal mining is dangerous because coal is found in underground layers. When the layers are close to the Earth's surface, miners peel back the earth to get to the coal. But when those layers are deeper, miners have to travel underground through tunnels to reach the coal.

Common causes of coal mining deaths include explosions and falls. Miners who don't get killed on the job often suffer from long-term health problems, including black lung. Black lung can lead to breathing difficulties and even death.

Improved technology and tougher laws have made coal mining a much safer job since the mid-1900s. But it's still dangerous. Since 1950 more than 10,000 coal miners have been killed in accidents in the United States alone.

Coal miners work in dark, dirty conditions.

POLAR EXPLORER

In the late 1800s and early 1900s brave explorers set out to map the North and South poles. American explorer Robert Peary was the first person to reach the North Pole in 1909. In 1911 a group led by Norwegian Roald Amundsen was first to reach the South Pole. Many others soon began exploring the poles, sometimes with tragic results. The freezing temperatures and icy terrain has killed or nearly killed hundreds of men.

FACT

In 1845 Sir John Franklin left England with two ships headed for the North Pole. Franklin's ships got stuck in the ice. An attempt to escape on foot failed. All 129 men died.

A DOOMED TREK

In 1912 Australian explorer Douglas Mawson led a team to do scientific research in Antarctica. One day, a hidden **chasm** opened under the snow. One of Mawson's two team members fell to his death. Their tent and nearly all their food fell with him. The two remaining men became hungry and weak. Soon Mawson went temporarily blind from the bright sun. His partner showed signs of insanity and eventually died. Mawson continued on, even though the skin peeled off his feet and his lips, and his nose split open. After three months, he finally made it back to base camp, only to learn that his ship had just left. He was forced to spend another year in Antarctica before finally returning home.

"My whole body is apparently rotting from want of proper nourishment—frostbitten fingertips, festerings, mucous membrane of nose gone, saliva glands of mouth refusing duty, skin coming off the whole body."

— Antarctic explorer Douglas Mawson

Douglas Mawson looks into the chasm his friend fell into.

chasm—a deep crack in the surface of the earth

19

EXPLOSIVE ORDNANCE DISPOSAL SPECIALIST

Explosives are a major threat to members of the American military. Many bombs go off when the weight of a person or car triggers them. One of the most dangerous jobs in the military is being an explosive **ordnance** disposal (E.O.D.) specialist. These military members identify explosives. Then they blow them up or **disarm** them safely. The **casualty** rate for E.O.D. specialists is double that of foot soldiers.

Often an E.O.D. specialist puts a small explosive next to the bomb and then explodes them both from a safe distance. Other times an E.O.D. specialist puts on a protective suit before approaching the bomb to disarm it.

Being an E.O.D. specialist is one of the most dangerous jobs in the military. But E.O.D. specialists have the ability to save countless civilians' and soldiers' lives.

ordnance—military weapons, ammunition, and maintenance equipment

disarm—to take a bomb apart so it cannot explode

casualty—someone who is injured, captured, killed, or missing in an accident, a disaster, or a war

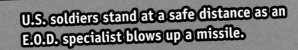
U.S. soldiers stand at a safe distance as an E.O.D. specialist blows up a missile.

KAMIKAZE PILOT

All military troops face the possibility of death. But kamikaze pilots faced certain death. These World War II (1939–1945) Japanese pilots purposely crashed airplanes carrying bombs. The goal was to crash the planes into enemy targets, causing the bombs to explode. The pilots were killed instantly. More than 1,000 kamikaze pilots lost their lives in the war.

NEVADA TEST SITE WORKER

During the **Cold War**, the United States and the Soviet Union were each afraid the other country would attack. For protection, each country built up a huge amount of weaponry. One type of weapon was the **nuclear bomb**.

From 1951 to 1962, the United States tested nuclear bombs by exploding them in an area near Las Vegas. This area became known as the Nevada Test Site. People living near the site were frightened by how life changed after the tests began. There was less wildlife. Thousands of sheep died.

The worst result was what happened to the workers at the site. They seemed fine at first. But over time many workers developed certain types of cancer. Many scientists believe the cancer was caused by **radiation** at the site. Now the U.S. government has a program to give money to former Nevada Test Site workers who get cancer. But for many of those workers, the money can't repair the damage to their health.

Cold War—a conflict between the United States and the Soviet Union (1947 to 1990); there was no fighting, but both sides made threats and developed weapons

nuclear bomb—a bomb that uses the power created by splitting atoms; nuclear bombs are powerful and can destroy large areas

radiation—tiny particles sent out from radioactive material; these particles can be harmful to living things

U.S. troops watch as a nuclear bomb explodes in the Nevada Test Site.

FACTORY WORKER

Factories became common in the late 1700s in the United States and Europe. At that time no laws existed to protect workers or keep them safe. Conditions in many factories were horrible by today's standards. Employees worked more than 12 hours a day. Many factories lacked heating systems to keep workers warm in the winter. There were no safety devices to protect workers from dangerous equipment. Steel workers worked dangerously close to tubs of hot, melted metal. And the fabric dust and particles in clothing factories gave workers lung problems.

Laws in the United States and other first world nations have made factory work much safer today. But conditions are still dangerous for workers in other places.

On November 24, 2012, a factory fire in Bangladesh killed 112 workers. The fire began on the first floor. Employees found themselves locked inside the eight-story building that had no emergency exits.

A young girl works at a cotton mill in North Carolina in the early 1900s.

THE TRIANGLE SHIRTWAIST FIRE

In 1911 the Triangle Shirtwaist Company factory in New York City had about 500 workers. Most were teenage girls. They worked in unsafe, overcrowded conditions. On March 25, a fire started near the top of the 10-story building. The building didn't have many exits. Even worse, some of the doors were locked from the outside, trapping workers inside. Fire truck ladders weren't tall enough to put out the blaze. As a result, 146 factory workers died in the fire. The tragedy led to law changes that made factories much safer.

In recent years, TV shows have shown that fishing is a dangerous job. Between 2000 and 2010, 124 out of every 100,000 fishing workers died on the job. The long hours, dangerous working conditions, and difficult work all bring great risks. Extreme weather also plays a role in the danger.

One reason why commercial fishing is so dangerous is that there are very few rules guiding the industry. Fishing boats must carry life rafts, emergency signals, and other supplies to help in an emergency. But there are no laws requiring that ships be in good condition or that workers go through emergency training. Between 2000 and 2010, more than half of all commercial fishing deaths were caused by problems with the ship. Often, ships sank.

A crab fisherman off the coast of California takes his catch from a trap.

Risky jobs have existed throughout history. As time goes on, many jobs get safer. Workers fight for better rights. New technologies help reduce risks, but they also create new dangerous jobs. After all, before the airplane was invented, who could have imagined kamikaze pilots? Before cars were invented, there were no race car drivers colliding in deadly crashes. It's only a matter of time before the next new dangerous job enters the scene.

TIMELINE

1750—TODAY
Common dangers faced by coal miners are explosions, falls, and respiratory diseases.

1750—TODAY
Factory workers deal with accidents, work-related diseases, and fires.

2700—1700 BC
Pyramid builders in Egypt suffered from broken bones, arthritis, and physical stress. Many builders were killed.

AD 600—1800
European kings and queens were frequently murdered.

330 BC—AD 450
Roman praegustatores risked illness or death by poisoning.

200 BC—AD 100
Roman gladiators often fought to the death for the enjoyment of spectators.

1800—TODAY
Waste pickers deal with exposure to toxic materials that cause asthma, cancer, and birth defects.

2000—TODAY
Commercial fishermen face high on-the-job risks for injury and death.

1990—TODAY
E.O.D. specialists deal with bomb explosions as part of their jobs.

1944—1945
Kamikaze pilots faced certain death when they crashed their planes into enemy targets.

1951—1962
Nevada Test Site workers often developed cancer due to radiation exposure from their jobs.

1845—1915
Polar explorers dealt with starvation, accidents, and exposure to cold.

1880—1914
Panama Canal construction workers were at risk of catching deadly diseases. They were also in danger from accidents on the job.

1911
The Triangle Shirtwaist Factory fire claimed 146 lives.

2003—TODAY
Cell phone tower repairmen risk on-the-job injuries and death. Ten workers died in 2004, 48 in 2005, and 18 in 2006.

GLOSSARY

arthritis (ar-THRY-tuhs)—a disease that makes people's bone joints swollen and painful

canal (kuh-NAL)—a channel that is dug across land; canals join bodies of water so that ships can travel between them

casualty (KAZH-oo-uhl-tee)—someone who is injured, captured, killed, or missing in an accident, a disaster, or a war

chasm (KAZ-uhm)—a deep crack in the surface of the earth

Cold War (KOHLD WOR)—a conflict between the United States and the Soviet Union (1947 to 1990); there was no fighting, but both sides made threats and developed weapons

disarm (dis-AHRM)—to take a bomb apart so that it cannot explode

nuclear bomb (NOO-klee-ur BOM)—a bomb that uses the power created by splitting atoms; these powerful weapons can destroy large areas

ordnance (ORD-nuhnss)—military weapons, ammunition, and maintenance equipment

pharaoh (FAIR-oh)—a king of ancient Egypt

radiation (ray-dee-AY-shuhn)—tiny particles sent out from radioactive material

tomb (TOOM)—a grave, room, or building that holds a dead body

toxic (TOK-sik)—poisonous

READ MORE

Gustaitis, Joseph. *Arctic Trucker.* Dirty and Dangerous Jobs. New York: Marshall Cavendish Benchmark, 2011.

Landau, Elaine. *Deadly High-risk Jobs.* Deadly and Dangerous. Minneapolis: Lerner Publications Company, 2013.

Nixon, James. *Infantry Soldiers.* The World's Most Dangerous Jobs. New York: Crabtree Pub., 2012.

INTERNET SITES

FactHound offers a safe, fun way to find Internet sites related to this book. All of the sites on FactHound have been researched by our staff.

Here's all you do:

Visit *www.facthound.com*

Type in this code: 9781476501277

 Check out projects, games and lots more at
www.capstonekids.com

INDEX